Nine Thorny Thickets

Nine Thorny Thickets

Selected poems by Dafydd ap Gwilym

in new arrangements by

ROLFE HUMPHRIES

with four translations by Jon Roush

The Kent State University Press
1969

Nine Thorny Thickets
Copyright © 1969 Rolfe Humphries
All rights reserved
Designed by Ruari McLean
for The Kent State University Press, Ohio
Printed in Great Britain by Westerham Press Ltd
Bound in Great Britain by The Wigmore Bindery Ltd, London

Library of Congress Card Catalog No. 68–27393

Other Works by Rolfe Humphries

Poetry
Europa and Other Poems and Sonnets
Out of the Jewel
The Summer Landscape
Forbid thy Ravens
The Wind of Time
Poems, Collected and New
Green Armor on Green Ground

Translations
Poet in New York (Garcia Lorca)
The Aeneid of Virgil
Gypsy Ballads (Garcia Lorca)
Ovid's Metamorphoses
Ovid's Art of Love
Satires of Juvenal
Selected Epigrams of Martial
Lucretius: The Way Things Are

Y mme'r llyfr hwn i Helen

Acknowledgments

Thanks are due The New Yorker, The Massachusetts Review, and The Colorado Quarterly for permission to reprint poems which first appeared in their pages; also to Indiana University Press for permission to use material which appeared in book form in the Collected Poems of Rolfe Humphries; and to the Amherst College Press for permission to use the four translations by Jon Roush from his Amherst College Honors Thesis #3, The Shape of the Harp. Thanks are also due Commander Publications for permission to use the musical arrangement by Johnny Mercer.

Contents

Introduction

Translations by Jon Roush

Nine Thorny Thickets set to music
by Johnny Mercer

Introduction

Any fool could whomp up biographical data about Dafydd ap Gwilym, whose name we might Anglicize as David Williamson, from the latest Encyclopedia Britannica, or some such source, and any fool interested in that kind of material can go thither to look it up. What I have to say is, briefly, to wit, as follows: this Welsh poet was, give or take a few years, a contemporary of Geoffrey Chaucer. He has about him much of the latter's early-morning freshness, but he is a much more adroit and accomplished technician. Unbound to bardic law, he is well-versed in bardic lore; uncommanded by courts, he feels free to go his own way, with a high respect for both tradition and innovation. A fellow of infinite resource and sagacity, like Kipling's Mr. Henry Albert Bivvens, A.B., he can bring over to his own tongue the convention of other languages; he has, for example, read Ovid to his profit and delight. The English poet who sounds most like him is Gerard Manley Hopkins; the earlier Catholic is unquestionably the less devout, but also less *angstvoll*, less pang-prone, more inclined to favor self-derision over flagellation. Dafydd also has in his make-up more than a trace of Skelton's ready rush and run of epithet, of Garcia Lorca's abrupt swerve and collision of metaphor and image.

Some of his effects derive from the promises he has to keep when he sets out. The Twenty-Four Official Welsh Meters make stipulations beside which the rules for sonnet, villanelle, sestina, are child's play. The Welsh did not, though they well might have, started off an *englyn* with the following stipulations:

1. Your first line must have eleven syllables.
2. Your second line must have five syllables.
3. You may use any beat you care to in these two lines.
4. Your second line must rhyme, not with the last syllable of the first, but with the eighth.
5. At least seven of the consonant-sounds in the first line must be repeated in the second.

We can imagine the protest a modern poet would raise about such rigid requirements stifling his genius, inhibiting his right to express his personality;

if he did not waste too much time doing this, he might produce

> Had we but world enough and time, this coyness,
> Lady, were no crime

His lines would conform to the specifications indicated above; his poem has already embarked on a road not taken by Marvell's, but it looks as if it might be going somewhere, toward demesnes of possibly greater interest than the untrammeled personality could devise. You can't, you see, be an utter witling, either as to sound or sense, if you accept some such imposition to begin with. What I refer to here is the Welsh insistence on *cynghanedd*, alliteration; without going into the detail of various types, this may range from something as simple as 'A *c*at may look at a *k*ing' to a much more involved, '*Scranton, scrawn-town's crone-tunes c*roon.' Shakespeare, who concedes the Welsh some rough homage in King Henry IV, has a good deal of it in his songs, –

> 'Full fathom five thy father lies,' or
> 'Fear no more the heat o' the sun
> Nor the furious winter's rages'

And when the Welsh base their line on a syllable count rather than an alternation of slack and stress, they permit, even encourage, the shift of emphasis, from the heavy regular iambic swat of

> 'The curfew tolls the knell of parting day'

to something as lovely as the lines from early in Twelfth Night, with a $3 \times 3 + 1$ pattern,

> 'O, it came o'er my ear like the sweet sound'

with the intricate interweaving of both vowel and consonant sound, the pauses, the secondary stresses, the use of *cynghanedd*. I suspect that some of Hopkins' rather top-lofty discussion of sprung rhythm was no more than his discovery of this kind of effect.

In rhyme, also, we have variety: the *cywydd* pattern, in which a stressed syllable rhymes with one unstressed, or the use of *proest* rhyming, which we now call slant-rhyme, or off-rhyme, and are familiar with in the work of Emily Dickinson, Wilfred Owen, W. H. Auden. In this kind of rhyme the Welsh may insist that only long syllables may rhyme with long syllables, diphthongs with diphthongs, short syllables with short – *oil* and *foul* is all right, or *vain* and *vine*, or *thin* and *then*, but not *bone* and *on*. You need not, they say, rhyme only at line-ends, on the right hand side of the poem; what is the matter with going from end into middle, or chiming the first syllable of line one with the last syllable of line six? William Barnes, as well as Hopkins, knew something of these matters, but now who knows anything about William Barnes? The people from whom we might expect these effects, Vernon Watkins, Dylan Thomas, Robert Graves, do not put them on display; this may be to keep the arcana from the profane eyes of the Sasenach, but I think it is more likely that they just plain do not know about them.

As for his themes, one thing Dafydd appears to enjoy very much is taking a conventional topic, and subjecting it to all sorts of variety. Take, for instance, the message genre, in which some creature is asked to convey to the admired or beloved personage the homage or wishes of the poet. This Dafydd can play straight, as he does in *The Blackbird* in this selection; or he can mock at the whole business, as he does in '*Take a Message*,' or – and this is his favorite response – he will use the convention, not so much for the sake of the message itself as for his delight in the bearer, *The Salmon*, or *The Titmouse*, and many other instances. Another pleasure for him is to take a stock property, like that of the Aubade, and substitute the homely touch for some of the pastoral rococo; or adapt something he has read in Ovid to a Welsh mise-en-scène; one of his *Three Porters*, for example, is very much like that Dipsas in Ovid's Amores I, viii. And who else, writing in English, is capable of his powers of variation? Who else can turn from the uproarious ribaldry of *The Thunder* to the deft, sly, subdued wit of *The Cat and The Mouse*? He will take a trite story, the old one about the lover who meets a girl in an inn, makes an assignation for later in the night, and gets into the wrong room, and turn this into something entirely fresh and new by transposing it into the first person, and by the striking epithet to which the use of *cynghanedd* prompts him. The old argument between the clerk and the soldier for the favors of the girl, a more than familiar theme with the Wandering Scholars, he retells, in his own

xiii

fashion, by letting the girl speak, very briefly indeed, on behalf of the soldier, who, in his own person, never gets a word in edgewise, while Dafydd discourses at length on the superior claims of the bard. It is, of course, something of a distortion to represent his 150-odd poems by a selection of forty, but these selections should give some idea. Who needs all of Wordsworth?

In these versions I have tried to show not only what Dafydd said, but how he went about saying it. In most of the poems, though by no means in all, I have used, I think more than other translators, the seven-syllable line of his *cywydd* originals, rhyming unstressed against stressed syllables frequently, and keeping in mind, always, the values of *cynghanedd*, though I can not possibly state that I have followed the literal requirements all the way through even one poem. A very few of these poems I did a long time ago, before I even knew of the Twenty-Four Official Meters, which I first learned in 1954 from Gwyn Williams' *Introduction to Welsh Poetry*, published by Faber & Faber a year earlier; among such items in this book is the 'Nine Thorny Thickets' piece, originally published in The New Yorker as *Night Song of Dafydd ap Gwilym*, where the composer Johnny Mercer saw it, liked it, and set it to music, also giving it the new title, which I like better than my own original. In at least one poem, the one about the poet in Morvith's arms, I have started out formally, but, as the emotion developed, let the poem break through the pattern; in some others, where I thought the poem would not be hopelessly spoiled by a longer line, I have used the *Gwawdodyn Hir*, or *Hir a Thoddaid* forms, and towards the end I have let his old age express itself in the short lines, the almost out-of-breath utterance, of the *Rhupunt* cadence.

Two girls' names I have phoneticised, or quasi-phoneticised; I'd hate to have the untutored American reader say Morfudd, rhyming with mud, or Did-goo, which suggests toilet-training. *Morvith* comes out all right; I am less happy with *Dovekie*, but *Dusky* is too dark, even for a brunette, and the alternative spelling, *Dovekey*, refers to an auk, not a dove. While I was about it, I also spelled Griffith in its more familiar form, not as Gruffydd. One or two place names, Anglesey, Glamorganshire, are translations; but I have kept Traeth Mawr, and Traeth Bach rather than say Big Beach and Little Beach, and in the poem where Dafydd is having such a good time recalling all the places where he was rejected by his lady-love, I have left the names exactly in his spelling, let the reader stumble over them as he may.

You are foolish if you expect here either definitive scholarship or Hinds & Noble interlinear fidelity to the words of the text. I have taken liberties egregious if not monstrous; I hope I have nowhere been licentious enough to impose myself on Dafydd. The fidelity is due the poem, not its syllable count, nor its number of lines, nor the proportion of upper-case to lower-case letters in the *Collected Works*. I know perfectly well that Dafydd did not quote Ovid in the original Latin, nor have a Welsh girl part from her lover at dawn with a half-remembered slogan from the Spanish (perhaps, though, she originally came from Provence, and might have done just that). I like to think that Dafydd would have been hugely delighted could he have known that almost six hundred years after his *floruit* somebody was performing such stunts for and with him. The cardinal principle to keep in mind, in this connection, is that your poet is in the same room with you, looking over your shoulder, or within call somewhere in the house, or strolling around your lawns and garden.

It is high time for translators to quit trying to inherit the earth by succumbing meekly to that tired old *traduttore-traditore* cliché, or the maybe-malice-made mot of Frost's that Poetry is that which gets lost in translation. How much poetry gets lost in the King James version of Psalm XXIII, or Job, 31–34, or the Song of Songs, which is Solomon's? How much poetry gets lost, in our own time, in Housman's rendition of Horace's *Diffugere nives*, or, for that matter, in Edmund Wilson's translation of Housman's own poem for his colleague, M. I. Jackson? Good ringing prose is also what gets lost in translation – ask your nearest friendly Loeb Classical Library journeyman. What was it Yeats wrote? –

> 'When I was young,
> I had not given a penny for a song
> Did not the poet sing it with such airs
> That one believed he had a sword upstairs.'

Translators should swashbuckle a bit more than we do. So here I am now, look you, a poet translating a poet, not some frayed but polite border functionary wearily exchanging the worn scrip of one republic for that of another.

My thanks to aiders and abetters begin next door with my neighbor, Miss Elsie Davies, who brought me, less than a year ago, some little Welsh periodical with eight or ten lines by Dafydd ap Gwilym, and thereby reawakened all my dormant interest in him. The enthusiasm of Mr. Howard Allen, Director of the Kent University Press, was very heartening; the National Translation Center, in Austin, Texas, supplied me valuable leads, notably to Professor Joseph P. Clancy, head of the English Department at Marymount Manhattan College, in New York City, with whom I have had interesting and profitable correspondence. His own *Medieval Welsh Lyrics*, published in 1965 by St. Martin's Press, is the best modern work in this field. A continent's width away, the people in the Robert Frost Library at Amherst College were prompt, courteous, efficacious and helpful, as they always were when I lived in the same town with them. Mrs. Grace Stearns Dilley very kindly checked out for me the resources of the Berkeley Public, and University of California libraries. Finally, my thanks conclude much nearer home than next door, with enormous gratitude to my wife, to whom this book is dedicated.

ROLFE HUMPHRIES

Woodside, California
St. David's Day, 1968

xvi

HOMAGE TO IFOR HAEL

Ifor, fortunate am I
In your generosity.
Not quite unrequited, you
Have me in your retinue,
Win my praises, pay me back
In good gold and splendid sack.

I baptize you by the name
Bountiful; no sword can tame
Such a soldier as you are,
Warrior, yet prisoner
Of a poet, princely fellow,
Best one for a bard to follow.

As the left hand yields in might
To the rigor of the right,
You, my lord, with no disbrace
To your honor, keep your place
Through my praise, which, near and far,
Testifies to what you are

Far as man or summer sun
Travels, far as wheat is sown,
Far as dewdrops glisten clear,
Far as eye can see, or ear
Hearken, far as Welsh is heard,
Far as grass-growth, song of bird.

Handsome, courteous, lavish lord,
Ifor, blessings on your sword!

THE BLACKBIRD

Blithe blackbird, early to sing
Across dew-fields at morning,
Chorister, caroller, heard
With rapture by every bird,
Moor-meadow-minstrel by choice,
But sometimes lifting the voice
Aloft from the walls of stone,
From a cliff-cold bastion.

From birch-tree or rowan-grove
We can hear your lauds of love,
Or in spring, from towers in town,
Arrayed in your glossy gown,
Wisdom-descanter, you spell
Lessons we ought to learn well.
Come from your stall in the choir
Gliding to Glamorganshire.

There is the Eden most blest,
The loveliest, the fairest,
Where my kinsman's mansions rise
From vineyards of Paradise.
There Ifor holds his estate
Tripling the fame of the great,
Nydd, Mordaf, Rhydderch, all three
Less in their boon, their bounty.

Fly to him, blackbird; kindly
Take him the message that I
Praise him for ever and ever,
Generous granter, giver
Of wealth beyond hoard and hold
Of wise King Solomon's gold.
Blackbird, take him my homage,
My honor to saint and sage.

'TAKE A MESSAGE'

Take a message to her, go,
Tell her, – wait a moment, though –
Best to take this rather slow.

Thinking it over further,
I say, gentle messenger,
Take this word from me to her,

Tell this delicate lady
That tomorrow I will be
At the – somewhere. Let me see,

Have her choose the when and where
And I'll try to meet her there
Be the weather foul or fair.

If she asks from whom you came,
Act confused, say 'What a shame!
He forgot to give his name.'

Or, as if you had not heard,
By her loveliness wit-blurred,
Stand there and don't say a word.

THE SALMON

Ocean-wave Esquire, Salmon,
God-graced, God-empowered one,
Of all sea-haunters, surely
The loveliest in the sea,
Whom blessed St. Curig's hymn
Guards as your deepness you swim
Through sea-weed, with never a fear
Of shallow, of wicked weir,
Or the harpoon, heart-cleaver,
Cast by Cain-thugs of the river.

As on land wild boar will flash
Through brake and brier and brush,
So, look you, shine and shimmer,
A torque of light in the water,
Salmon, haste, but guardedly
Lest resentful watchers see.
Upstream going, upstream go,
Where, more fair than the swallow
In flight, the white wave over,
You come to her, you find her.

Fear no rock, no coracle
Where an angling man may dwell
With wet line, with barbed hook,
But where river shrinks to brook
Just beyond the sliding height
Where the foam-white down-rush brightens,
Turn where under the osiers
Stillness hardly more than stirs
And lake is a quilt of quiet,
No fruitfall, no footfall yet,
No red apple from orchard
On the green level of yard.

Salmon-esquire, summon her
Away from her lord and master;
But she will have known before
The call has come to her door,
And you will see her standing
Tall by the river-landing.
Which one she is you will know
By the skin as white as snow,
By the rose-cheek, the gold ring,
Which – alas! – she is wearing.

You will know her from the rest
By her perfection of breast,
By her raven-dark-night hair,
By all her blitheness, fair
As Luned, the gentle maiden
Of the Lady of the Fountain.
Swim by her, heedful, slow,
Giving her, as you go,
My true acknowledgment,
Linger until she has leant
Over the water, then leap
High to her, out of the deep,

Then, erudite advocate,
Tell her my pitiful state
With Merlin tongue subtlety,
Depose to her that I die,
Discourse and dwell on my pain
Over and over again,
Selecting the language well
Weave her in your salmon-spell,
With eloquent leap, fall, rise,
Make the tears brim up in her eyes.

Instruct her that goddesses chaste
Keep lovers too long unblest;
Vows are no doubt very fine,
But I need fulfillment of mine.
Wherefore and why postpone
The joys that we both might own?
Expend, my good counsellor,
Every ounce of your legal lore
In the final analysis,
The last word, briefly, this –

Murder me, darling, outright
Or leave your husband tonight.

THE TITMOUSE

Coal-black head and craichy cry,
Tiny titmouse friend, Goodbye,
Time for you to get you gone
Northward to my lovely one,
Find, in Meirion, her house,
Light there, and from May-bright boughs,
Sing the message of my love
Softly down the hawthorn grove.

Deft in darting, you can bridge
Waterway and woodland hedge,
Blacks and greens and whites and blues
In the raiment of your hues,
You're no flap-wing, loud-mouth bird,
But your *Sweetie, Sweetie*'s heard
By all listeners in love,
And your heart is very brave.

Off, be off, like wind be gone
To my girl in Meirion,
Praise her for her comeliness
In her golden bower, address
Greeting to her, but remind her
She is mine; don't let me find her
License-loosed, or lewdly led
To some other fellow's bed.

From your hawk-unhaunted perch
On the boughs of oak or birch,
Trusty troubadour-minstrel
Carol such enchanting spell
That she knows you share with me
In avowal completely
Our devoted psalm to her,
Little seer-sage-chirruper.

Tell her, Dafydd in the south
Hath her praises in his mouth,
On his lips, the livelong day,
Living only to obey
Her awaited bidding; fly
Quickly back with her reply,
Come! – so I shall surely break
Shafts of longing for her sake,
Rise, and travel toward the bright
Rampart-bastion of her sight.

LOVE AT FIRST SIGHT

Ah, my darling, my dear,
That wonderful golden hair,
Light-cloud around neck and ear,
And that white-gold radiancy,
That loveliness of the body,
Shame the gold-white of the day.
And the music-mellow voice,
Sweeter than organ-tone
In St. Deiniol's evensong,
Makes vesper-hour rejoice,
But no seven odes could cure
Even one wound of my seven.

Where she moves, there is Heaven,
Though folk say Anglesey,
But how can it Heaven be
With Dian-archery?
Not under any sky
Goeth her healer-brother;
Not under any star
Groweth, to balsam heart,
Blossom to heal this hurt.
No smith had ever the skill
To forge that singing steel,
To whet that sharp an edge.

I am all grief, all groan,
Alive, a-lost, alone,
While she, in company
Of Mary, Heaven's queen,
Walketh her way serene
In an evening light that pales
The light of the evening star
Over northwestern Wales.
I am Sorrow's black serf, dark churl
Bound to a gamestress girl,
A spirit broken and bound
As I cry from my wrack, my wound.

9

MORVITH'S PENITENT PILGRIMAGE

Pledge of promise in the risen sun!
Morvith, my love, my maidenly nun,
Hath her penitent pilgrimage begun
With flowers for having killed a man.
I was her victim, she my murderess,
Whom Saint David bless; bless her, Saint John.

O, all ye rip-rift rioters, be
Ebb-level, every estuary
A pool for her paths past Anglesey,
O Traeth Mawr and O Traeth Bach, may she
Get easy going; I'd gladly give a farm
To see her pass Barmouth in safety.

And all ye lovely golden rivers,
Deep Dovey, whose each ninth wave shivers,
Rheidiol, Aeron, be her givers,
Like lingering or laughing lovers,
Kind to her wending-way along the coast,
Be for her almost backward movers.

Mary, mother of all happiness,
Hear my sea-bird criminal confess
Her sin to sea, to Mynyw moor; bless
Her contrite heart; boon me no redress,
Grant her Thy grace; ah, Mary, robed in blue,
I speak true. I do forgive her. Yes.

IN MORVITH'S ARMS,
THE FIRST TIME

Praised beyond all Enids be
Lady Morvith, my lovely.
I burn with more than a fire
From the torch-light of her hair,
And yet, her touch as it fell
Was almost-virgin-gentle.

Around my neck white arms went;
Her red lips were impatient.
That kind of kissing has come,
So more than mild, most seldom.
Her poet-prisoner, frail
In her wine-sweet body-gaol,
So I, though I do not tell
All truth of the miracle.

So, in the bonds of the bright
Of her arms, all snow-drift white,
She was imprisoning me
All courtly, lightly, gently.
Who would want to stir
Out of her hold and halter?
Who would want to move
Out of that lock-up love?

And how could a man do better
Than submit to this fetter,
These gyves, this white-snow-gentle
Link and loop of the circle,
Chain and charm of the shackle,
Feather-threat of the throttle,
Wrist-hold, kiss-bold tether
Keeping us close together?

Each man thinks he knows best
Of Arthur's loveliest –
Tegau of the golden breast,
Dyfyr of the golden hair,
Enid, the radiant girl,
Daughter of Yniwl's Earl.

But I, Dafydd the dark,
The swarthy one, soot-sallow,
The too black crow-skin fellow
Rise over them all, and follow
Companioned only with
My marvel, my Morvith,
So follow, and so fare
Toward that wider air
Rimmed by the gold-white arc.

How bountiful! How blest!

AUBADE

It seemed as if we did not sleep
One wink that night; I was sighing deep.
The cruellest judge in the costliest court
Could not condemn a night so short.
We had the light out, but I know,
Each time I turned, a radiant glow
Suffused the room, and shining snow
Alit from Heaven's candle-fires
Illuminated our desires.

But the last time I held her, strong,
Excited, closest, very long,
Something started going wrong.
The edge of dawn's despotic veil
Showed at the eastern window-pale
And there it was, – the morning light!
Gwen was seized with a fearful fright,
Became an apparition, cried,
'Get up, go now with God, go hide!

'Love is a salt, a gall, a rue,
A vinegar-vintage. *Dos y Ddw*,
Vaya con Dios, quickly, too!'
'Ah, not yet, never yet, my love;
The stars and moon still shine above.'
'Then why do the raucous ravens talk
With such a loud insistent squawk?'
'Crows always cry like that, when fleas
Nibble their ankles, nip their knees.'

13

'And why do the dogs yip, yammer, yell?'
'They think they've caught a fox's smell.'
'Poet, the wisdom of a fool
Offers poor counsel as a rule.
Open the door, open it wide
As fast as you can, and leap outside.
The dogs are fierce when they get untied.'
'The woods are only a bound from here,
And I can outjump a deer, my dear!'

'But tell me, best beloved of men,
Will you come again? Will you come again?'
'Gwen, you know I'm your nightingale,
And I'll be with you, without fail,
When the cloud is cloak, and the dark is sky,
And when the night comes, so will I.'

THE DREAM

It must have been near morning
When I dreamed I was hunting
My hounds beside me, all good
Trail-trackers, into a wood.
There I unleashed them, and they,
With bounding, belling, and bay,
Were up and off and away,

Pursuing a foam-white hind
Who fled them, fleet as a wind,
Down dale, up hill, and over
Two ridges of forest fir
Till footsore, weary and lame,
Tired enough to be tame,
At last to my side she came.

I woke with a start; it seemed
This had meant more than I dreamed,
So I sought an interpreter,
A sybil. I said to her,
'Wise one, rede me aright
The truth that comes to your sight
About my dream of the night.'

'Young man, your fortune is good
Your hunting-hounds in the wood
Are your messengers of love;
You will catch your wild roe alive,
And the girl will come to your side
White as foam-froth on the tide,
To be your blessing and bride.'

ONE SAVING PLACE

What wooer ever walked through frost and snow,
Through rain and wind, as I in sorrow?
My two feet took me to a tryst in Meirch,
No luck; I swam and waded the Eleirch,
No golden loveliness, no glimpse of her;
Night or day, I came no nearer
Except in Bleddyn's arbors, where I sighed
When she refused me, as she did beside
Maesalga's murmuring water-tide.
I crossed the river, Bergul, and went on
Beyond its threatening voices; I have gone
Through the mountain-pass of Meibion,
Came to Camallt, dark in my despair,
For one vision of her golden hair.
All for nothing. I've looked down from Rhiw,
All for nothing but a valley view,
Kept on going, on my journey through
Cyfylfaen's gorge, with rock and boulder,
Where I had thought to ermine-cloak her shoulder.
Never; not here, there, thither, thence,
Could I ever find her presence.
Eagerly on summer days I'd go
Brushing my way through Cwcwll hollow,
Never stopped, continued, skirting
Gastell Gwrgan and its ring
Where the red-winged blackbirds sing,
Tramped across fields where goslings feed
Below the cat-tail and the reed.
I have limped my way, a weary hound,
In shadow of the walls that bound
Adail Heilyn's broken ground.
I have hidden, like a friar,
In Ifor's Court, among the choir,
Sought to seek my sweet one there,
But there was no sign of her.
On both sides of Nant-y-glo
There's no vale, no valley, no
Stick or stump where I failed to go,

Only Gwynn of the Mist for guide,
Without Ovid at my side.

Gwenn-y-Talwrn! – there I found
My hand close on hers, on ground
Where no grass was ever green,
Where not even a shrub was seen,
There at last I made the bed
For my Morvith, my moon-maid,
Underneath the dark leaf-cloak
Woven by saplings of an oak.
Bitter, if a man must move
On his journeys without love.
Bitter, if soul's pilgrimage
Must be like the body's rage,
Must go down the desolate road
Midway through the darkling wood.

THE GIRLS OF LLANBADARN

I am one of passion's asses,
Plague on all these parish lasses!
Though I long for them like mad,
Not one female have I had,
Not a one in all my life,
Virgin, damsel, hag, or wife.
What maliciousness, what lack,
What does make them turn their back?
Would it be a shame to be
In a bower of leaves with me?
No one's ever been so bitched,
So bewildered, so bewitched
Saving Garwy's lunatics
By their foul fantastic tricks.
So I fall in love, I do,
Every day, with one or two,
Get no closer, any day,
Than an arrow's length away.
Every single Sunday, I,
Llanbadarn can testify,
Go to church and take my stand
With my plumed hat in my hand,
Make my reverence to the altar,
Find the right page in my psalter,
Turn my back on holy God,
Face the girls, and wink, and nod
For a long, long time, and look
Over feather, at the folk.
Suddenly, what do I hear?
A stage whisper, all too clear,
A girl's voice, and her companion
Isn't slow at catching on?
'See that simple fellow there,
Pale and with his sister's hair
Giving me those leering looks
Wickeder than any crook's?'
'Don't you think that he's sincere?'
Asks the other in her ear.

'All I'll give him is *Get out !*
Let the Devil take the lout!'
Pretty payment, in return
For the love with which I burn.
Burn for what? The bright girl's gift
Offers me the shortest shrift.
I must give them up, resign
These fear-troubled hopes of mine:
Better be a hermit, thief,
Anything, to bring relief.
Oh, strange lesson, that I must
Go companionless and lost,
Go because I looked too long,
I, who loved the power of song.

THE WINDOW

Everything was going well –
I, in this woodland tangle,
Sang a serenade, and crept
Closer, where her beauty slept,
Just beyond the leaves, blow
The oaken casement window.

'Open one small pane of glass,
Kiss me,' I implored the lass.
Neither spell nor serenade
Roused this most reluctant maid.
She refused. I thought, *Well, well,*
Here's an ungentle jewel!

And the window, splinter-old,
Fly-speck-spotted, maggot-holed,
Blocked me. May I never age
Like that window! In my rage
I remembered Melwas, who
Dragged the girl he loved right through.

Melwas came from Caerlleon,
Feared nothing in his passion.
Still, I am, to my regret,
Not of Melwas's stature yet.
All I did was peak and pine
For the loveliness not mine.

Knowing well I could not hoist
Her between a jamb and joist,
With no star-lit hope of her,
I developed dire anger,
Raged at those blank walls that rose
Barricades to lip and nose.

Night and sleeplessness, below
This let of lattice window.
May the devil's crowbar pry –
Dafydd, don't blaspheme! – so I
Found a saw, and cut my way
To the place my loved one lay.

THE THREE PORTERS OF JEALOUSY

His Loutship, named Jealousy,
Hath in service porters three.
Surely, surely, I should know,
Didn't they scare me hollow?
One, a son of bitch's whelp
With a yap, a yowl, a yelp,
Bell-bawling, dew-lapped dog,
Less of a bull than a hog;
Two, a door whose retching rasp
Grates and grinds with ghoulish gasp,
Without medicine of oil,
Ghost-gargle of death-rattle.

Three, worst of all, an old crone,
The ugliest ever known,
A bag of bad bones in bed,
A saddle-snouted head,
Riddled with every disease,
A cotquean sleeping with fleas,
Early to bed, and early
To rise, complaining, surly,
Hip, hand, knee, elbow, shoulder
All mean miseries to her.
Malice, malevolence, spite
Season her appetite.

Last Wednesday I went my way
Where His Loutship's lady lay.
Cheerily, I wended on
Toward the portal of that prison,
Grateful for the grace of dark,
When out, with never a bark
Of courteous, kind warning,
Who should angrily spring
But that slobber-slaver hound?
With a leap, a growl, and a bound
He tore my coat from my back
In his foul-fiend-fanged attack.

But I'm fond enough for more,
I lift the latch of the door,
It clicks a little, I push
Through the blessed boon of a hush,
And then, – what an idiot shriek!
What a raucous rasp and a squeak,
A rust-rot wrack of a cough,
As if the hinge broke off,
And a concentrated gabble
Which all of the geese in Hell
And Rome could never equal,
Never combine to cackle.

Next, a hiccup and quaver,
'O Master, Master, Master,
The door must be ajar ('ck!),
Can't you hear the watchdog bark?'
No use in trying to stay
After that, I'm on my way,
I had best be gone, I think.
I can smell the hell-hound stink
As over the sill I go
Along the wall's long shadow,
Chilled to the marrow, and poor,
No love-trove, no such treasure.

I shoot over my shoulder
A Parthian arrow at her,
And it finds her heart, and she
Fires back her fondness for me,
But out comes old Green Eye
With his hag from her husks, and from sty
His cursed cur, and they all
Banish me beyond recall.

But God has ever a house
For his poet, under green boughs
Where rivers run, and a home
In the cool coves of the coombe,
And His mercy, loving and good
Shadows my meadow and wood.

TALE OF A WAYSIDE INN

With one servant, I went down
To a sportive sort of town
Where a Welshman might secure
Comely welcome, and pleasure.
There we found the book to sign
In the inn, and ordered wine.

But whatever did I see
But the loveliest lady
Blooming beautiful and bright,
Blossom stemming from sunlight,
Graceful as the gossamer.
I said, 'Let me banquet her!'
Feasting's a fine way, it seems,
For fulfilling young men's dreams.

So, unshy, she took her seat
At my side, and we did eat,
Sipped our wine, and smiled and dallied
Like a man and maid, new-married.
Bold I was, but whispering,
And the others heard nothing.

Troth and tryst we pledged, to keep
When the others were asleep.
I should find my way, and come
Through the darkness to her room.
Love would haul my steps aright
Down the hallways of the night;
Love would steer my steps, – alas,
This was not what came to pass.

For, by some outrageous miss,
What I got was not a kiss,
But a stubble-whiskered cheek
And a triple whiskey-reek,
Not one Englishman, but three,
(What a Holy Trinity!),
Diccon, 'Enry, Jerk-off Jack,
Each one pillowed on his pack.

One of them let out a yell,
'What's that thing I think I smell?
There's a Welshman must have hid
In the closet or under t' bed,
Come to cut our throats with knives,
Guard your wallets and your lives,
They're all thieves, beyond all doubt,
Throw the bloody bugger out!'

None too nimble for my need,
First I found how shins will bleed
When you bark them in your haste
On a stool that's been misplaced
By some ostler-stupid fool,
Then the sawney of a stool
Squealed its pig-stuck tattle-tale
After my departing trail.

By good luck, I never got
Wet-foot from the chamber-pot.
That was all I saved myself,
Knocked my noggin on a shelf,
Overturned the table-trestles,
Down came all the pans and kettles.
As I dove to outer dark,
All the dogs began to bark.

Asses bray, and scullions rouse
Every sleeper in the house.
I could hear the hunt come round me,
Scowl-faced scoundrels, till they found me.
I could feel their stones and sticks,
So I clasped my crucifix,
Jesu, Jesu, Jesu dear,
Don't let people catch me here!

Since my prayer was strong, I came
Through the mercy of His name
Safely to my room at last,
All my perils over-passed.
No girl's love to ease my plight,
Only God's that dreadful night,
To the saints be brought the praise,
And the Good Lord mend my wicked ways.

LOVE AT FIRST SIGHT,
A BRUNETTE THIS TIME

Lord of spear and lord of men,
Evan, courageous captain,
Son of Griffith, host or guest,
Generous above the best,
I recall a night I spent
In your halls, with merriment
All around me, mead, gold, ale, –
What a wealth of wine-wassail!

Only, since then, it's been hard
For your fever-fretted bard
To put down one stave of song
Or to sleep a wink, night-long,
Since he set his eyes on her,
Dovekie, your dark-browed daughter.
She'll not love me, heart of stone,
Scornful in her stone mansion.

Not one Stoic sage could be
Cold-hearted to her beauty,
Face as wonder-white as snow,
Dark the raven hair and brow,
Darker than a brooch of jet
Or an ebon amulet,
But like snow again is she
In her church-chill chastity.

Peredwr, as I recall,
Loved a lordly girl, as tall.
Just as beautiful, but more
Tender toward her warrior.
Peredwr recalled a place
Where the wild hawk left a trace
Of a blackbird's murder, blood
Crimsoning snow-floor in wood.

There, by Yseult's grove, I see
Symbol, emblem, imagery
Spread across the snow-blue white,
Black her hair as darkest night,
Forehead, as her husband boasts
Snowdrift-white as Arctic coasts
And upon her cheeks, the low
Blood-fade, sunset's afterglow.

In my wayward rounds, I've played
Being judge, assizes made,
Given sentence, settled suit,
Now it's my own case that's moot;
Let my crowd of critics pass
Verdict on this court-caught lass,
Is it worth my fret, my fever,
To keep living just for her?

AN INVITATION

Dovekie, of the soft dark hair,
I invite you, come and share
With your love, my radiant one,
My dark glade in Mynafon.

No vile victuals for your feast,
Swill unfit for man or beast,
Gluey gruel, stringy meat
Lean as Lenten fasters eat.

Rest assured that I have not
Asked one single Saxon sot
With his loud-mouthed company,
Drunk for their majority.

No, my dear; the wine we need
Will be nothing more than mead,
And for dancing-music, – hush!
Hear the nightingale and thrush.

Nine majestic trees of birch
Pillar our rotunda church
Rising to its belfry tower
From white clover, heaven's flour.

There two people, sometimes four,
Lie untroubled, hour by hour,
Watch the deer come down for grain,
Hear the meadow-lark's refrain.

Where the blackbird builds his nest,
Where the fledgling falcons feast,
There our passion-Eden lies,
There our perfect Paradise.

Where no hedgerow-haunting lout
Ever holds his talons out,
Begging for his cheese or bread,
Where the light from overhead

Filters down to still waters
Through an air that never stirs,
Glow-worm eyes, and cheek wave-white,
Come with me, and spend our night.

THE HATEFUL HUSBAND

'Tis sorrow and pain,
'Tis endless chagrin
For Dafydd to gain
His dark-haired girl.
Her house is a gaol,
Her turnkey a vile,
Sour, yellow-eyed, pale,
Odious churl.

She cannot go out
Unless he's about,
The blackguard, the lout,
The stingy boor.
The look in her eye
Of fondness for me –
God bless her bounty ! –
He can't endure.

I know he hates play :
The greenwood in May,
The birds' roundelay
Are not for him.
The cuckoo, I know,
He'd never allow
To sing on his bough,
Light on his limb

The flash of the wing,
The swell of the song,
Harp-music playing
Draw his black looks.
The hounds in full cry,
A race-horse of bay,
He cannot enjoy
More than the pox.

My heart would be glad
At seeing him laid
All gray in his shroud;
How could I grieve?
Should he die this year,
I'd give him with cheer
Good oak for his bier,
Sods for his grave.

O starling, O swift,
Go soaring aloft,
Come down to the croft
By Dovekie's home.
This message give her,
Tell her I love her,
And I will have her,
All in good time.

FROM A WELL-WISHER

So you're on your way to go
Overseas to fight the foe,
Though I can't remember when
You belonged with fighting men
In a company like these
Guardsmen of great generous Rhys,
Brothers, cousins, battle-falcons, –
Mary, bless St. David's sons!

Men, you have a yellow-jacket
In your columns, if you let
This girl-fighter, poet-loather,
March with you, the mangy cur.
Left, right, left – one ear, one eye,
And that always cocked to spy
Some girl's leg, and never shut
If there's anything to loot.

And his lackeys, what a troop!
Rheum-red, senile-stinking group,
Whom I fear, if they close in,
Worse than death, or mortal sin.
If he boards, this swill-fed pig,
Battle-barkentine or brig,
Not one ship a sail will swell,
Not one venture down the Channel.

Heave the wretch, the weasel's rump,
Overboard, or make him jump
Off the taffrail, walk the plank,
No one but himself to thank.
If nine waves suck down the fool
In the salt-wheel spin of whirlpool,
Then I'd owe you, generous wave,
Nearly everything I have.

If by luck he gets to France,
May misfortune be his chance,
May he find the net, the snare
Finely-meshed to gin him there;
May the men with cross-bows pull
Bowstrings back, and split his skull,
Drive bolt two into his lush
Fennel-feathered whisker-bush.

Twelve disastrous dooms descend
On his body, end to end;
Never let his muzzle scent
Good home-fragrant airs of Ghent.
That will teach him, bards are known
As fine folk to leave alone.
Let the red-hand black-heart die
To the paean of my outcry.

THE THUNDER

Sweet words and a scented bed
Underneath birchleaves I had,
And a pretty girl, whose play
Crushed the lovely leaves of May
In her fingers' wantonry, –
Why not come to bed with me?

She, brown-eyed, and I were laid
Under birch-leaf counterspread
When a peal of thunder struck,
Clearly, 'twas no time of luck,
For the thunder, like a hammer,
Pounded clamor, clamor, clamor.

Lightning spat, and rivers poured
Cruel cataracts – dear Lord!
Down the dale my darling fled,
Handkerchief held over head,
We were parted, torn asunder
By rain-rush and threat of thunder.

Fire would crackle, fume and splutter
In its battle with the water;
All the bulls of Bashan, or
Builth, at least, began to roar,
Not to mention battering-rams
Getting in a few good slams.

Wagons rumbling cobblestones
By the thousands shook my bones,
Oaks were tossed against the sky,
A red witch commenced to cry,
What a hateful, hideous hag! –
Brandishing her rattle-bag.

Jesus Christ, behind a cloud,
Chanted *Dies Irae* loud,
Blasting on His trump, the way
I'd expect on Judgment Day,
And the thunder roars and bellows,
Laughing at the sky's pale yellows.

No one sky-fart, nor a few
Fired petards could scare us two,
But the blend in all of this
Wind-and-water synthesis
Of two basic excrements,
Most insistent, most intense.

This is what the crack of dawn
Meant that day, a sweetheart gone,
Downpour over glade and glen,
Panic in the roar of rain,
Separation, and the old
Solitude of lonesome cold.

THE BOG

The poet stumbles in fright –
Dark is the cold-bog night;
Dark, – will no rescuer search?
Dark, – for God's sake, bring a torch!
Dark, darker, darkest, – how soon
Can Dafydd expect to find
The sun in this bitter wind?

And even if I should be found,
This is an odious land,
Where strangers, lying in wait,
Murder the men they hate.
Better, or worse, had I drowned
In that whirlpool-bog, hell bound,
With my horse stuck dead in the mud
On the floor of that foul flood?

The fish of Gwynn of the Mist
Are swimmers, more or less lost,
In that fen, that pit, that bog
Between the moor and the crag,
Where ghosts and their children are
In the lake of vinegar,
Where swine wash the wallow-mud
Out of snouts in this black blood.

And my good Carnarvon hose
Are ruined; God only knows
How it ever came to pass
We fell into this morass.
The cold numbed my horse, poor lout,
But he warmed up floundering out.
So now we are safe again.
Bless you, my favorite fen!

THE WIND

Rush of the noisy wind roars over sky
Keeping on course, Oh, very deftly,
Marvellous of movement, going by;
Tell me, tell me, might and majesty,
From what northern valley, high and far,
You come where we are with loud outcry.

Go and find the girl I dearly love
Across the silver of Aeron wave,
Do not fear the little hunchback knave
Whose foul tongue keeps me exile. I crave
Your vengeance from on high; on him let fall
Doom-dread of your call; hearken, and save,

Save me. Nest-ravager, breaker of bough,
Whom no sheriff halts, no troops allow
Any way but onward, pride and power
The warrant, the authority. O thou
Destroyer and preserver, hear our prayer,
Let our cry, our care, invoke you now.

No mortal questioner has ever found
Sources of your start, your journey's end;
Fire never burned you or water drowned,
Darkness could not ever countermand
Your over-ocean rampage, or your sweep,
A seven-land leap at every bound.

Night-trumpeter, mast-breaker, laugher,
Blusterer, seed-sower, winnower
Of wheat before the sheaves of winter,
Soft-silent as an oar in feather,
Evader, cunning pauser when you go
Into lying low, sly subsider,

Be no more than a stir in the air,
Breeze-breath only. Halt and hover there
Where my Morvith of the golden hair
Dwells, descend, whisper to her, swear
In the name of every holiness
All my dark distress, my cry, my care.

THE WINTER

Across North Wales
The snowflakes wander,
A swarm of white bees.
Over the woods
A cold veil lies.
A load of chalk
Bows down the trees.

No undergrowth
Without its wool,
No field unsheeted;
No path is left
Through any field;
On every stump
White flour is milled.

Will someone tell me
What angels lift
Planks in the flour-loft
Floor of heaven
Shaking down dust?
An angel's cloak
Is cold quicksilver.

And here below
The big drifts blow,
Blow and billow
Across the heather
Like swollen bellies.
The frozen foam
Falls in fleeces.

Out of my house
I will not stir
For any girl
To have my coat
Look like a miller's
Or stuck with feathers
Of eider down.

What a great fall
Lies on my country!
A wide wall, stretching
One sea to the other,
Greater and graver
Than the sea's graveyard.
When will rain come?

NINE THORNY THICKETS

All this I was doing
Over a girl,
In loneliness going
Across the bare moor
And through the blind night
In the pitch of the darkness,
Lost from the high road.

Through many ridged fields
Down slopes that were soggy,
Over stubble and furrow
With stumble and sorrow,
Through nine thorny thickets,
By ruined old forts
To the brow of the mountain,

And missing the bogs
And their green habitation
Whose hateful companions
Circled around me,
A fighter betrayed
In the thick of the battle,
A man in a gaol.

But worse than the bogs
And all desolation
Were the spirits of evil
Circling around me,
And my crossing and praying,
My charming and rhyme
Of little avail.

This took a long time:
But at last I looked up
And there were the stars!
Like cherries they were
In the orchards of night,
All yellow and red,
All shining and bright,

The sparks of the bonfires
Of seven dear saints,
The gems of the host
In the harness of heaven,
The pickets of embers
Whose orbits are long
And wind cannot take them.

I stopped in my tracks,
And 'Look you,' I said,
'This is over and done.
She will have to be told,
God forgive me the telling,
I'll travel no more
To the door of her dwelling
Through any such going,
Nor blunt my good axe
On the face of the stone.'

44

THE RIGHT TRUE VOCATION
(*Vade Mecum* for a Nun)

I am foolish, I am fond,
Waste my love on one beyond
Any courtly call of mine.
In pale cheeks her dark eyes shine,
Seldom raised, a votaress
Vowed to God. Nevertheless,
Let me question, catechize,
Draw out her devout replies.

Dearly beloved daughter,
Listen to your minister.
Is it true, my eight-hued star,
That a female saint you are,
True that all your lauds belong
To cloister-cling, psalter-song?
Cresses, water, crusts of bread, –
These preserve your maidenhead?

Child, your simple soul must be
In most heinous heresy.
Leave your orisons, and break
Every bead, for Christ's sweet sake!
Quit your cell for the green grove,
Nunneries go ill with love,
And your maidenhood, take my word,
Is betrayal of Our Lord,

Our Lord Love, for whom we dress
All in green, for graciousness,
Whispering our vows in church
Underneath responsive birch,
Or in hawthorn chapel, where
Ovid is our thurifer,
There, from forest fathers, win
Absolution for our sin.

God and all His saints above
Pardon and encourage love,
And no single shire or shrine
Gives redemption's blood and wine.
Can it matter where a maid
Saves her soul, in woodland shade,
Walks abroad or kneels at home,
Nentyrch, Santiago, Rome?

THE COWARD

'Langorous, daylight-lovely,
Count pebbles, learn what's due me;
Dark-browed, gold-jewelled one, sing
An accurate accounting.
Haven't I given you praise
For complexion, figure and ways?'

'Dafydd, I've pardoned you long –
It's you who are in the wrong.
Let's give things their proper due,
Coward's the title for you.
I'm for no fellow to have
Excepting one who is brave.'

'Girl of the gossamer hair,
I may not be bold to bare
My breast in battle, forsooth,
But what saith Ovid to youth?
Aye, and more often than once –
Militat omnis amans.

'Furthermore, where are the charms
Of some roigh minion-at-arms?
Your wonderful warrior
Is a bother, a boor, a bore,
A savage, an uncontrolled
Lover of wars and the cold.

'If he hears of a new campaign,
There he goes, off again
To fight the Scotch or the French?
What does he want of a wench?
All he desires, the fond fool,
Is to find his name on the roll.

'If he comes home from the wars,
Racked and riddled with scars,
He'll have no tenderness left,
No love, no longing to lift
Anything else but a lance.
Don't give the churl any chance.

'Don't trust a fellow whose field
Is bound by saber and shield.
Grievous to trust him; the churl
Cares more for a horse than a girl,
Uncouth, discourteous ape
Whose method of love is rape.

'Now I, with livelier tongue,
Offer you lovely song,
Woven, invisible,
From the scholarship of my skill.
Were you mine, two monarchies
Could not tempt me from your eyes.'

THE BAD, BAD GIRL

What a handsome couple, we
Trysting in the greenery,
She a comely woman, I,
Poet Dafydd, graceful, shy.
May-month was the time, the scene
Where a hillside grew its green
Shadowing a slope; I gave
Kisses that she seemed to crave.
Two to one, the kissing-score
In her favor. I gave more.

But as on and on we went
She appeared more discontent.
When I heard her talk so bold,
Wanton-witch-wise, uncontrolled,
I was frightened; haven't I
Told you I was rather shy?
I withdrew into my shell,
Fearful of each syllable,
Tried to hide my thoughts from her
By jaunty jibber-jabber.

All in vain! My fate was spun,
This new color-scheme begun.
'Dafydd, what a boor and clown
You must be! Have you come down
All this way, without one stir
Of the flesh? Don't you remember
I was never cold nor coy?
What's the matter with you, boy?'
'Fair one, you must know I love you,
But I've no intent to have you.'

49

'Do you think I came here to
Look at trees, or gaze at you?
No such thing! I'd hoped to shed
My provoking maidenhead.'
'But a virgin still you'll be
When you leave, for all of me.
Mary helping me, you'll go
Purer than the driven snow.
Be assured I'll not submit,
Wise through having lost my wit.

'Furthermore, I want no part
Of your father's angry heart.'
'Dafydd, this is stupid stuff;
Don't you think it's safe enough
Where the grass lies deep on lea,
Where we'll let what will be be?'
'Kinsfolk give black looks; and, worse,
There's the great Archdeacon's curse,
Excommunication, fine,
Forty shillings on the line.'

'Nasty-niggard, churlish-cheap,
How can forty shillings keep
Any Welshman back, who might
Purchase such a dear delight?'
'But what if I did not bring
That much money this morning?'
'Borrow it from me, and pay
With a song, or as you may.'
I gave in, said my *Yea, sure,*
And enjoyed perfect pleasure.

THE CAT AND THE MOUSE

She's as unreliable
As the mouse once was, who fell
From a beam into the beer,
Newly-brewed November cheer,
Would have drunk-drowned in the vat,
But was salvaged by a cat,
By a good gray cat, who leapt
Lightly down, and lithely kept
That unfortunate inept

From the death he might have known.
Not that cats are over-prone
In their love of mice as such,
But this rodent promised much,
Took his Bible oath, and vowed
He would show his gratitude
Soon as he was lifted free,
Pay his proper heftage-fee
Happily and handsomely.

But no sooner was one eye
Half-unblinked, one whisker dry,
When he scuttled off, – Goodbye!
Down his old familiar path
Back to plaster, back to lath.
'Mouse, you've gone too far; behave,
Keep the promise that you gave.'
'Don't be gullible, gray cat.
Is there any reason that

When I'm drunk, the things I say
Are dependable next day
Or an oath I swore in beer
Can be held to bind me here?'
There are lessons in this, Gwen:
Mice conduct themselves like men,
Men like mice; but then, again –
Do I need to say it twice? –
Girls are less like cats than mice.

IN PRAISE OF SUMMER

Father of the heat and hum,
Father of blossom and bloom,
Of growth in the woodland, tall
Tower to wanderers all,
Waker of earth from slumber,
Maker of song and of stir,
For heath and for hedge the bold
Bronze bracken, the sunlit gold
Of broom, bush, tree, abounding
In the lavishry of our king.

Wherever he moves or dwells
Are the ways of miracles,
Swallow-sweep, lark-lift, nestling
Whir-noise, new on the wing,
Hay-bright, hive-bold, from the dawn
Till the dew of might comes down,
The prophet in Druid green
Arranges, arrays the scene,
Which August, that threatener,
Makes promise to pilfer.

Tell me, Summer, let me know
To what other land you go?
May not poet-friend presume
To ask whither, Sire of Bloom?

'Poet,' sang Summer, 'be still!
Tongue-flattery is evil.
Thrall am I as much as thane
Possessor of no mortmain
Beyond green tent and tangle.
Banished, I must go to dwell
In Annwfn, far below
Wind-wound, whistle-sword snow.
June-jester, cuckoo-courtier,
Will retinue me thither.'

53

Farewell, father, kindly king!
Poets' praise and bards' blessing
Attend and accompany
The royal dormancy.
During the bright banks' fade
The sun succumbs to the shade
And the music, mute in the hall,
Patiently at the portal

Waits till the door swings wide
And our prince comes proud outside,
Then harp, horn, voice, flute, drum, bell
To fullest volume swelling
To the bright emblazoning
Hailing our warm-heart king
His Majesty the Sun
In his right restoration.

THE THRUSH

Listen! The thrush is singing to me now,
From steeple-spire, or from a topmost bough,
His anticles of love, his theme the *How*,
The *Wherefore*, and the *Why*, of lovers' vow.
May evenings in the fields, maidens can hear
Silver serenade, as the light fails,
And lovers, waiting for the dearer dark,
Tell each other *Hark!* all over Wales.

Yesterday, underneath a birch-tree lying,
I kept quite still, for I could hear him trying
His opening bars and trills, the measure dying,
Rising again, full volume, verifying
My motion: he should read the lesson clear,
From the lectern bless us with his voice
At matins, preen his feathers like a clerk
Smoothing cassock, – 'Brethren all, rejoice,

'Rejoice, and be exceeding glad, for I,
Love's loyalest lay-reader, testify
Among you, of the gloriously high
Power of his perfect principality.'
He knows the songs of other birds as well;
He could quote you words from Ovid's *Art
Of Love;* most musical, his speech bewrays
Something of the preacher in his heart.

Preceptor and precentor, May-minstrel,
He gives instruction to the folk who dwell,
Ignoring hymnals, on each syllable
Issued from the pulpit-perch of hazel.
And how divinely, with what angel grace,
Modulating changes, seraph-wise,
The sermon lifts, lilts, softens, till mean hear
Solo from choir-loft in Paradise.

55

AN ELEGY FOR GRIFFITH,
SON OF ABBA

In the old orchard by the whitewashed wall
Before the time of red-gold apple-fall
Outdoors, or gold-red hearthe-fire autumnal,
Where nightingales in summer dark would call
From groves of green, what catastrophic change
From delight! How strangely ruined, all!

Powys a fine fair fruit-hold used to be,
With drinking-horns held high for revelry,
Where taverns flowed red wine, and the pear-tree
Gave bloom and fruit, promise, reality,
Till that black-hearted bowman's cruel craft
Loosed his quarrel-shaft, clove, most foully

The temple-bones of Griffith, where there clung
The fine-spun gold hair of our lord of song,
Our nightingale, our summer bee, whose humming
Did no man ever dight or dab of wrong,
Abba's good son, Gwenwynwyn's singing lark.
For this deed of dark, let him be hung,

Hung high, whatever death his devil chose
To deal, skull-splitting poultryman, base blows
From sword, or battle-axe, or bolt, – who knows?
Griffith has gone, and with his going goes
Our music-mirth, our angel, and our saint.
Whose cheek pales fast, faint with fading rose.

TALK WITH A SHADOW

Yesterday, under birch-leaf green,
I stood waiting in the rain
Like a young damn fool for Gwen
Who, I thought, was like Helen.
Some one, something, dismally
Loomed up there in front of me.
It might not intend me ill,
But I crossed myself from evil,

Said, 'Speak! Tell me, if you can,
Who you are, what kind of man?'
'I'm your shadow, Dafydd; be
Silent, do not hinder me
From the truth I mean to tell,
I am kindly, wish you well,
I'm your image, I abide
Naked, almost, at your side.'

'What a lie! To me you look
Like some rag-tag kind of crook
Husband-hired, a spook scarecrow
Following me where I go.'
'How you wrong me! I am not
Partner in such evil plot.'
'Ghost-goat, don't apologize!
Can't you see that I have eyes?

Utter loneliness would be
Better than your company,
Shag-shank shepherd, heron-lank,
Fish-fed from some soggy bank,
Palmer-pale, rag-wrapped in black,
With a hump along your back,
Mothmeal blanket, and a hood
Soiled from farmyard muck or mud.'

'But I follow everywhere;
Where you travel, I must fare,
Unsubstantial, that is true,
But I know a thing or two
I could tell, I could expose,
More than anybody knows.'
'Satan-shit on you! I've not
Ever played Iscariot,

Chucked a stone at dog or hen,
Ever tried to scare children.'
'But suppose I said you had?
You'd be a gone goose, my lad.'
'Let me give you some advice:
Think this over more than twice,
Or sew up your lips with twine
For your benefit and mine.'

THE MIRROR

I used to think my face was good
Or fair at least, but having viewed
My mirror-features, now I find
I am compelled to change my mind.
I have grown ugly. Enid's brow
(I love her so!) has changed me now

Into a specter, gaunt and wan,
My rosiness of cheek is gone,
My color comes all gray and sallow
Marked with streaks of jaundice yellow;
My nose looks sharp enough to make
A razor with, for Jesus' sake!

My eyes' bright beams are blind and dull,
My hair comes out by the handful.
My face is dark as dragon-spew
Or basilisk-spat. What can you do,
Dafydd, unless your mirror lie,
Except resign yourself and die?

A loathsome lodestone, this moon-glass
Draws the needle of my compass
By its sickly light, witch-made,
Out of good day toward evil shade,
Dream-pallor, cold, unstayed, and lost
In brittle brotherhood with frost.

THE RUIN

Nothing but a hovel now
Between moorland and meadow,
Once the owners saw in you
A comely cottage, bright, new,
Now roof, rafters, ridge-pole, all
Broken down by a broken wall.

A day of delight was once there
For me, long ago, no care
When I had a glimpse of her
Fair in an ingle-corner.
Beside each other we lay
In the delight of that day.

Her forearm, snowflake-lovely,
Softly white, pillowing me,
proferred a pleasant pattern
For me to give in my turn,
And that was our blessing for
The new-cut lintel and door.

'Now the wild wind, wailing by,
Crashes with curse and with cry
Against my stones, a tempest
Born and bred in the East,
Or south ram-batterers break
The shelter that folk forsake.'

Life is illusion and grief;
A tile whirls off, as a leaf
Or a lath goes sailing, high
In the keening of kite-kill cry.
Could it be, our couch once stood
Sturdily under that wood?

'Pillar and post, it would seem
Now you are less than a dream.
Are you that, or only the lost
Wreck of a riddle, rune-ghost?'

'Dafydd, the cross on their graves
Marks what little it saves,
Says, *They did well in their lives.*'

HIS OLD AGE

Grief and love's dart
Harrass and hurt
My heavy heart.
So, I am old.

Once, young and gay,
I went my way,
No such dismay
Balking my boldness.

For my Lord Love
Valiant I strove,
Minstrel, word-weaver,
True at my trade.

I had my store,
My share and more
Of girls adoring.
I am fast fading

Woefully now,
Blight on my brow,
Gloom where the glow
Used to be bright.

Gone the proud air,
Passion and power
Dim to despair,
Darkness and night.

Cheated of choice,
Muscle and voice
Renounce rejoicing
Once and for all.

I was a lover
Famous forever, –
All that is over,
Still, if she'd call –

HIS OWN FUNERAL

Below gossamer you stand
With lily-forehead garland –
Who will deliver the lover
From this death-body ever?
I dare no blood-feud, I go
Before I, with vengeance-vow,
Am killing your kith and kin,
In my own turn, assassin.

Far from us both, bright jewel,
Be any crime so cruel!
But soon my grave must be laid
Under growth of the greenwood glade,
And the pillars of my church
Be rowan and ash, young birch,
And some gay garment-weaver
Plait my pall from the clover.

And all the flowers of the wood
Fashion me a fragrant shroud,
And a thousand sea-gulls bear
The eight fir-boughs of my bier,
And you own twin nightingales,
The loveliest-voiced in Wales,
Each side of the altar, be
Choir for the ceremony.

But the Mass must also be heard
In languages other than bird,
In the learned Latin, sung
By brothers amorous, young,
On whose lips there cannot rise
The chanting of jealousies.
Llan Eos, have haven-grave
For a life laid low by love.

And may God keep true His tryst
With His paltry poet's dust,
Offering and sacrifice
Chord his path to Paradise;
Orison, organ, intone
Invoking intercession,
And the cuckoo, at the last,
Chant his *Ite, missa est !*

It is a pleasure and privilege to include in this book the four translations that follow, made by Jon Roush in connection with his project for Final Honors in English at Amherst College in 1959, subsequently published, with some of Mr. Roush's own poems, in a brochure entitled *The Shape of the Harp*, issued by Amherst College Press in 1960. *The Birch House* and *The Mass in the Grove* are musts in any collection of Dafydd ap Gwilym; *The Goose Closet* is the only version I know of in English verse; and besides all that, Mr. Roush's translations are as fine as any I know.

R.H.

THE RATTLE BAG

One time of most leisurely eulogy,
A summer morn, I trysted under a tree
Between the mountain and the meadow
With my maiden of words of melting snow.
She came to me, I won't contest a thing,
Promised moon to the promised mooring.
We sat together, suitable matter,
Discussing our thoughts on this and that
(And on my age-old major demand)
I and this glorious girl reasoned.
We sere sitting so, she stayed shy still,
Slowly perceiving our love's preamble.
For a long hour we lay together,
Hiding all harm, winning mead with her,
When a clamor came (cold food for longing)
From a stinking-faced foul crying thing.
From a bag's bottom a vile boiling we heard,
Played by a beast disguised as a shepherd.
He had with him a hatefully gagging
Juiceless-horned brittle-jawed rattle bag,
Which this yellow paunched little visitor
Played on his shabby scabby shank's spur.
There, before we reached love's hoped-for end,
The fearful worthy girl was frightened.
When she, her breast wretchedly wounded,
Heard the strident winnowed stones, she fled.
Under Christ, it was not a Christian tune
But a cold name on a white mountain:
Squawking sack at the end of a stick,
Bell with a stone and pebble stomach,
Bulging chattering English belly
Quaking in ox-hide, a crow off-key,
Basket bouncing three thousand beetles,
Tumultuous black-sack cauldron of spells,
Keeper of the field, the straw's foul saint,
Black skinned hag, shake-splinter pregnant,
Hateful its hack to an old roebuck,
Devil bell, in its crotch a stake stuck,

Scar-crested stone-carting pebble bellow.
Let it make buckles for a scarecrow,
And may coldness catch the scattering churl
(Amen!) who scared away my girl.

DAFYDD AP GWILYM

THE BIRCH HOUSE*

I've loved a girl grown tall and fair,
From far-once to now to forever.
I went to her (hear my woe),
Hoping to salve my sorrow
With a wistful whispered wish;
Her reply was plain and knavish:
'I'll never love a homeless man,
Be he boor or bard or baron.'
I thought I knew her answer
And made a house of love for her,
Weary work below a birch tree,
A porch approach straight and stately,
A door adorned with dignity,
House for Merlin, home for Mary,
Roofed with leaves and softest twigs,
Tallow-gummy tiles of sprigs;
And now, my ample tempting manse
I'll lease to two lusty tenants,
Two with only one language,
Two birds of love to make one sage,
Cordial thrushes, sparrow-speckled,
Two sprightly-pinioned poets held
High in holy purity,
Birds of Paradise, my plea.
Seven poems they'll daily sing
To fit the vines' entwining,
And I'll record each seven
Whole in the hill, one by one.
To the girl I've coveted
To keep my house, make my bed:
If you refuse my entreaty
On the hill of the birchwood tree,
I swear to all this fearful vow –
I'll build for other girls tomorrow!

DAFYDD AP GWILYM

*Acknowledgment is made to *The Massachusetts Review* (Fall 1959), in which this poem first appeared.

THE GOOSE CLOSET

One time, a woeful evening,
I sought a woman, a worthy thing,
But lost my way in wandering
Through dangle-thicket dingles.

'Why wait so long; why so late?
So patient for one so passionate.'

'My Gold, you know the field too well;
Sin, my Sun, is never punctual.'

It was then we heard the husband near,
A lion's eyes, to lay the snare,
To lunge and launch the wrathful chase –
Remorseless man, bloody malice –
Bilked by his wife, his bailiwick:
One mighty hero, by God and relic!
I knew flight before his ire;
She knew the brown dream of fear.

'Slow is the pain of the spear all-piercing;
I pray this night to hear
My blood-weeping weapons blear
Songs you sang when she was near.'

I fled to a shed and shut the door.
(Heart restored, return to horror!)
There was a goose, beak-bright girded,
And I, sunk deep in darkness, said,
'Though feathers are thicker beside me,
This soft bed's no better for safety.'
The old goose raised her nose, releasing
From her down her hidden offspring.
She flew at my cloak front and back,
Bitter nurse with no elegiac,
And her tiny family all fell in,
Puking havoc with beaks wide open.

Until dawn this goose was my sister
With ten gentle chicks to comfort her,
(Seven worse than when were at hand
I, the woman, and words from the husband)
Her foolish-feathered knuckle-neck
Plucking, buffeting, pecking.
She held the club of lordship stiff
Over Caer Gwyr, and I, her caitiff,
I ran from the waggling goose,
Warned by the battle-cry bilious
Coming from the creaking-breast body,
A witch's choler to kill me.

DAFYDD AP GWILYM

THE MASS IN THE GROVE*

Today I lolled below a mantle
Of leaves grown over by green hazel
And heard, as dawn drew on the dingle,
The cock thrush's skillful canticle.
He drew a dancing stanza's design,
Alluring sign and fluent symbol.

Distant his nest, wisdom his nature;
The brown-downed herald had flown this far
From rich and refined Carmarthenshire
To the heavens of the valley here.
So verbose for one without a visa,
He had come to please a girl, I'm sure.

Yes, it was Morfudd who sent him hence,
May's foster-son of song-filled cadence
Adorned all around with ornaments:
Boughs of wild flowers and mild May scents
Clung so like a cloak that I couldn't tell
The wings from the mantle from the winds.

There was nothing here, by the Great God,
But shining gold in the altar shade.
I listened to every lucid word,
The lengthy rite delightfully read
To the waiting natives without a halt,
The faultless words in a faultless wood.

Then the lifting on the ash tree hill
Of leafy holy wafers awhile,
And the slender fluent nightingale,
The forest border's winsome minstrel,
Joins the thrush in a lively litany,
Singing bright as any sanctus bell.

Rising, the sacrifice was alive
And bold in brake and heaven above.
Invoking God the Father, they gave
The votive chalice and chant of love.
I am at peace in the sound of the psalm
Bred in the calm of the birch-bough grove.

DAFYDD AP GWILYM

*Acknowledgment is made to *The Massachusetts Review* (Fall 1959), in which this poem first appeared.

Nine Thorny Thickets

set to music

by Johnny Mercer

Nine Thorny Thickets

Lyric by ROLFE HUMPHRIES
(after Dafydd ap Gwilym 1320 - 80)

Music by JOHNNY MERCER

INTRODUCTION

VERSE #1

All this I was do – ing o – ver a girl, in lone – li –ness

go – ing a – cross the bare moor and through the blind night in the

rit. - - -

pitch of the dark-ness, lost from the hi-gh road ____

VERSE #2

Though man-y ridged fields, down slopes that were sog-gy, ____ o-ver

stub-ble and fur-row with stum-ble and sor-row, ____ through

nine thorn-y thick-ets, by ru-ined old forts, to the brow of the

lit – tle a – vail._____ This took a long

time, but at last I looked up and there were the stars

Solo

like cher – ries they were_____ in the

or – chard of night_____ all yel – low and red_____ all

shin — ing   and   bright _____

VERSE #6

The   sparks of   the   bon - fires   for   sev — en   dear   saints,   the

gems   of   the   host   in   the   har — ness   of   heaven, _____

_____   the   pick — ets   of   em — bers   whose   or — bits   are

long and wind can-not take them _____ (and)

wind can-not take them. _____

VERSE #7

I stopped in my tracks, "Look you," I said "This is

o — ver and done. She will have to be told God for —